the

Featherweight

Ads

D. Philipp Kaiser

First Published September 2007
by Darrel P. Kaiser
Huntsville, AL

Darrel Kaiser Books
www.DarrelKaiserBooks.com
Green Mountain, Huntsville, AL
Email: Dar-Bet@att.net

Second Edition 2014

Dedication

This book, as well as any future books I may write, is dedicated to the memory of my recently passed beloved and treasured wife,

BETTY MAY KAISER

Her caring love, constant companionship, unwavering support, and unlimited patience inspired and guided me as we walked our Lord's path together, both as Best Friends for over 45 years, and as one as Man and Wife for over 40 years.

My Betty, my one and only love, still and always. My eternal thanks… Soon we will meet again.

The Author

D. Philipp Kaiser is a sewing machine collector and was a professional sewing machine technician. His collection includes five or six Featherweights and Sewhandys in various stages of restoration, plus a variety of German and American antique machines.

Along with this book, he has also written and published five books covering German and Russian History, Politics, Religion, and Ancestry; a few novels, one book on the beautiful and unique Watercolor quilts of Betty Kaiser; a book on electrical systems troubleshooting; a book on the designs and patents of the SINGER 221/222 Featherweight Machine; and two books on the original SEWHANDY Sewing Machine.

For more information on his other books, visit his website at

www.DarrelKaiserBooks.com

Novels by **D. Philipp Kaiser**
in his Volga Ancestor series:

March to the Volga

Dreams on the Volga

Escape to the Volga

Tree of the Volga

Harvest of the Volga

Will of the Volga

Table of Contents

the

Featherweight

Ads

the
Featherweight Ads

Newspapers and magazines made, and still make, a lot of their money from running advertisements. Lucky for us....for if it had not been profitable, these ads would not exist. These old newspaper and magazine ads give us informative and enjoyable snapshots of what went on in the past. While it was not their intent, the publishers have preserved a very rich source of information for later generations

This book is a collection of 80 Featherweight ads that ran in papers and magazines across the United States. This is just a small sample of the ones printed during this period. If you have some that are not shown here, email me copies and I will add them to the next edition. There are also 10 pages of Featherweight brochures in the collection.

The collection starts with an ad from November 1934. This ad is the very first print advertising use of the "featherweight" name that I have discovered. The last ad is from 39 years later in December 1973. It probably ran to clear out old "new" SINGER 221 machines.

Some of the ads are extremely detailed. Others are no more than the very simple classified ads. I have included even the simple ones because they illustrate the selling price in a particular month and year.

Many of these ads ran on different dates, and the listed date is just one of those publication dates.

I found both the ad designs and prices very interesting. I hope you have as much fun as I did taking the trip back down memory lane. Enjoy.

A few famous quotes about advertising...

"The most truthful part of a newspaper is the advertisements."
~Thomas Jefferson

"Advertising says to people, 'Here's what we've got. Here's what it will do for you. Here's how to get it."
~Leo Burnett

"Advertising is the greatest art form of the 20th century."
~Leo Burnett

"Advertising is the genie which is transforming America into a place of comfort, luxury and ease for millions."
~William Allen White

1934 - 1939

LIFT IT
with one Finger

The new featherweight Singer
Electric Portable

● It's so light. Take it along whenever there is something new to be made. The new Singer Portable Electric, easy to use, and easy to own through the Singer "Make-It-Yourself" Plan. This newly developed Singer is so compact, so swift, so quiet, so efficient in operation that you can use it for every sewing need.

See it today, or have our Bonded Representative bring you one to try.

In its specially constructed case, it's no larger than an overnight bag.

SINGER
SEWING MACHINE CO.

MAKE IT YOURSELF ON A SINGER

"LIFT IT *with one Finger*" promoted the lightness of the Featherweight while obviously an exaggeration

This November 1934 ad was the first use of the "featherweight" name that I have found

"THE Perfect Gift!"

The "FEATHERWEIGHT" name now in all caps in this Christmas 1935 ad... Yours for only $3 a month

THE FEATHERWEIGHT
SINGER ELECTRIC

Light, compact, easy to carry, easy to use, and easy for you to give. Small down payment delivers it for Christmas—terms as low as-

$3 A MONTH

Has all mechanical features of larger, more expensive machines; fits into smart leatherette carrying case. Ideal for wife, mother—college and business girls. Complete sewing course included.

"Singer makes your CHRISTMAS CHOOSING easy! TEN PRACTICAL GIFTS FOR BUSY HOMEMAKERS"

Singer makes your

CHRISTMAS CHOOSING *easy!*

TEN PRACTICAL GIFTS FOR BUSY HOMEMAKERS

SINGER QUEEN ANNE. One of the most beautiful sewing machines ever made, the graceful Singer Queen Anne is equipped with silent, gear-driven electric head, Singerlight, reliable speed control, many "extras"...$10 down; choice of easy payments.

SINGER FEATHERWEIGHT PORTABLE. A favorite with busy younger women—extremely portable—weighs but 11 lbs., 1 oz.! Full rotary—forms perfect lock-stitch, forward or backward. Complete in smart luggage-type carrying case, only $6 down.

SINGER VACUUM CLEANER. For thorough cleaning without effort, it's the *Singer Vacuum Cleaner!* Features: Smart streamlines, powerful two-speed motor, revolving brush, headlight. Automatic Cord Control in De Luxe Model, $5 down; convenient terms.

SINGER HAND CLEANER. She'll use it *often* for cleaning stair carpets, draperies, furniture, car interiors. Unusually powerful suction. Accessories (small extra charge) include extension tubes, mothproofer, paint sprayer. $3 down; terms to suit your convenience.

December 1939

9

1940 - 1949

Featherweight Sewing Machine Has All Features

At last! The sewing machine that does everything but lay the pattern on the material is on the market. It's the new featherweight White Rotary electric now being shown at the White Electric Sales.

This convenient new machine, which will do everything that a cabinet model does, is compactly fitted into a smart airplane luggage case which can be easily carried from room to room.

The machine, which weighs 10 pounds less than the ordinary portable, achieves its lightness from a new featherweight metal. A boon to the women who do their own sewing this tricky new portable sews backwards as well as forwards, has a built-in sewing light, a hemstitching attachment, tension and stitch control devise, and a hinged presser foot which automatically adjusts to various thickness of fabric.

And as an added feature of convenience—you can pack your newly made spring wardrobe in the smart machine case when you leave for your Easter week-end trip.

February 27, 1940
Feature Article on the new Featherweight, except this is the *other one* made by the White Sewing Machine Company

"My Christmas Shopping's in the Bag"
The WAR is still on! No Featherweight, in fact no machines featured at all....

Sewing Boxes; Sewing Kits. Handsome boxes in fascinating shapes and patterns; fitted or unfitted. $1.00 up. Handy kits, including cases for service men and women; from 50c.

Sewing Stools. A real convenience! Any friend of yours who owns a sewing machine would love one! Right height for sewing. Unfitted, $16.00. Fitted, with tray and supplies; $19.50.

Handsome Sewing Cabinets. A gift in the grand manner! Each one is fitted with sewing supplies; each is an attractive piece of furniture in its own right! Several models; from $15.95.

"My Christmas Shopping's in the Bag

—THANKS TO MY SINGER SEWING CENTER!"*

Ladies—you can echo those joyous words! Hurry to your Singer Center—for the grandest gifts that ever made eyes light up like Christmas tree candles! See a preview on this page—get out your shopping list—and go!

*The address of your local Singer Sewing Center is listed in your telephone directory under "Singer Sewing Machine Co."

E-Z-Make Snuggle Dolls. Little girls love them madly. You'll enjoy making and dressing them! Dolls stand 12" tall when finished. Materials and directions; $1 for each doll.

Fresh, Crisp Neckwear. Trim dickeys, beloved by school girls and career girls alike; from $1.00. Collar-and-cuff sets, tailored and crisp or frilly and feminine; from $1.00.

Luscious Costume Flowers. For the pillow's hair, belt, or lapel. From 50c. Sachets, a nice extra or "stocking" present; 10c up.

Soft, Pretty Scarfs. Any woman is glad to see one of these come out of the Christmas wrappings! Gay prints. Paisleys, florals, solid colors; from $1.00.

Need a Singer?

If you've hoped that Santa will have a Singer at the foot of your tree this year—start hustling now!

New Singers are available—though the supply is limited and you may have to wait your turn.

Reconditioned Singers—rebuilt to give you real Singer quality and performance.

Rental Singers. Rent one by the month for home use; by the hour at your Singer Center!

Pretty-Plus-Practical Aprons. Some of these charmers are all made up; from 99c. And some, very special ones, are semi-made; you add appliqué and trim. $1.50.

Fashion-Wise Handbags. And as useful as they are good-looking—big enough to hold knitting or sewing. In lovely shades of long-wearing leather; from $4.95.

Cuddlee Cut-Ups. You make these quickly, easily! Makings; 50c each. And when you buy 4, you get the Merry-Go-Round free!

SINGER

SEWING CENTERS EVERYWHERE
Singer Sewing Machine Co.

Copyright 1944 and 1945 by The Singer Mfg. Co. All rights reserved for all countries.

Christmas 1944

"LOOK! THEY'RE HERE!"

World War II in Europe is over... Singer Sewing Machines are back in production

- A Modern Desk—With a Smooth-Stitching Singer Electric Inside!
- Convenient and Efficient—The Singer Featherweight Portable Electric!

LOOK! THEY'RE HERE!

- A Singer Electric in a Beautiful Period Cabinet!
- One of Singer's attractive Economy Cabinet Electrics!

Order your new Singer Sewing Machine Now!

3,500,000 women plan to get new sewing machines— don't you be left out!

As this is being written, Singer factories are starting to make new Singer Sewing Machines again!

It's good news—exciting news—news you've waited a long time to hear!

You—and three and a half million other women!

Yes—that's how many are planning to buy new sewing machines, a recent survey shows.

Go now to your local Singer Sewing Center and order the machine of your dreams—a Singer!

For, though production may be limited at first, the demand won't be! Some of those 3½ million women may have to wait a long time! Don't let that happen to you!

Get your order in today. Be among the first to have your new Singer carried proudly over your threshold!

SINGER
SEWING MACHINE COMPANY

FOR YOUR PROTECTION. Singer sewing machines are sold only through Singer Sewing Centers—never through department stores or other outlets. Singer Sewing Centers are listed in your phone book under Singer Sewing Machine Company.

May 1945

"At last – I can order my new Singer Sewing Machine!"
World War II in Europe is over... Singer Sewing Machines are available to order again

"At last—I can order my new Singer Sewing Machine!"

As this is being written, Singer factories are starting to make new Singer Sewing Machines again!

It's good news—exciting news—news you waited a long time to hear!

So if your heart's set on a new Singer, order it *now* at your Singer Sewing Center (Listed in your phone book under Singer Sewing Machine Company).

Though production may be limited at first, remember, the demand *won't* be! To be among the first to have your new Singer carried proudly over your threshold—get your order in today.

You'll be set to make wonderful clothes for yourself and the children —all at sweet, low cost! Mending chores become so much easier. And your smooth-running Singer can do wonders with draperies ... curtains ...slip covers for your house!

SINGER DREAMS COME TRUE!

Smart clothes for you: pretty things for the children.

Curtains, draperies, slip covers—so easy, so moneysaving to make!

Just one of the period cabinet styles you may choose for your Singer Electric.

A Singer Economy Budget Electric— well-built, attractive, a real value!

An 11-pound wonder—the tuckaway Singer Portable Electric.

Smart, streamlined styles, too— made for modern decorating schemes.

SEWING CENTER

FOR YOUR PROTECTION: Singer Sewing Machine Company sells its machines only through Sewing Centers identified by the Red "S" trade-mark on the window—never through department stores or other sewing machine dealers.

SINGER

SEWING MACHINE COMPANY

Copyright U. S. A. 1945, by The Singer Manufacturing Co.

May 1945

"Gifts from your Singer Sewing Center"

1947

"<u>Another</u> date? Gosh, Sis ...what that Singer Sewing Center did for you!"

SINGER SEWING CENTERS
THERE'S ONE NEAR YOU TO SERVE YOU

1947

"It was just a storage room – before I took lessons at the SINGER SEWING CENTER!"

"It was just a storage room—before I took those lessons at the SINGER SEWING CENTER!"

SINGER SEWING CENTERS

May 1948

"The Famous Singer Featherweight PORTABLE"

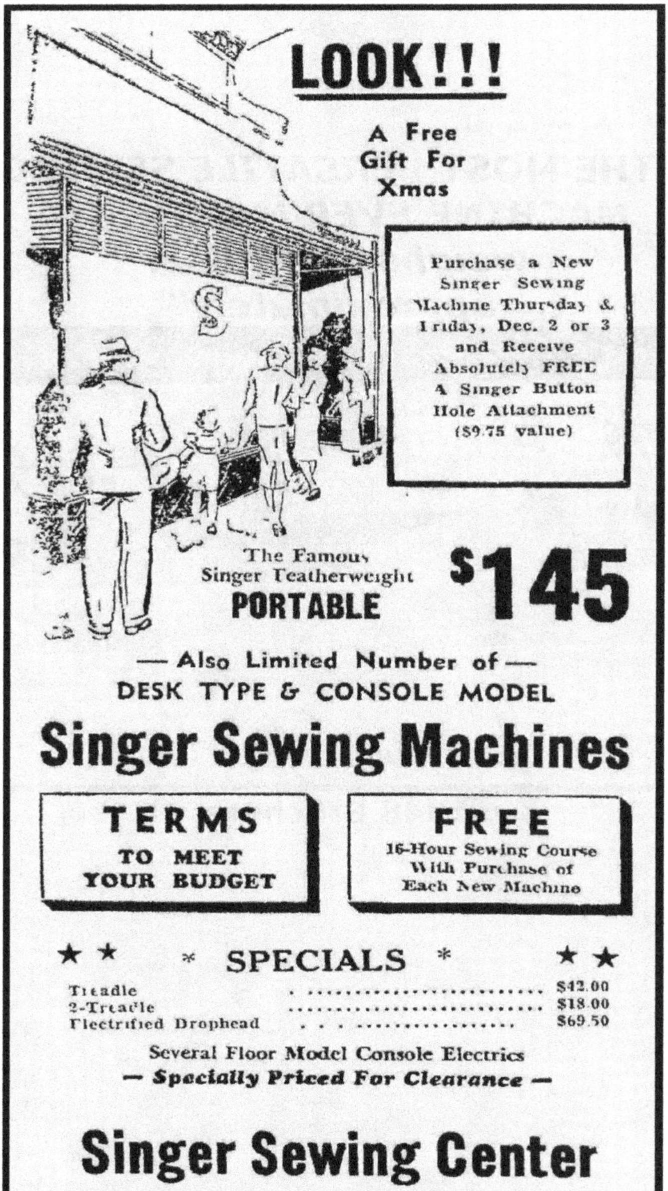

December 1948

"THE MOST *VERSATILE* SEWING MACHINE *EVER MADE!*
weighs 11lbs 4oz!
approximately"

1948 Brochure

"WHOA! HERE'S WHERE WE DO OUR CHRISTMAS SHOPPING!"

December 1948

"Now! Have the latest styles for <u>half</u> what they'd cost in a store!"

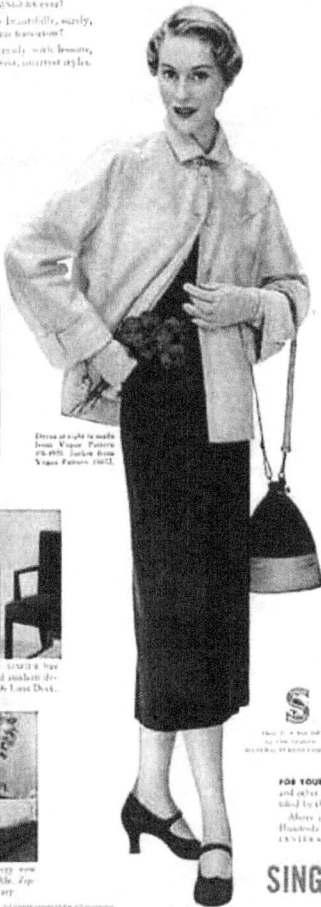

Now! Have the latest styles for half what they'd cost in a store!

A BEAUTIFUL NEW SINGER WILL HELP YOU DO IT!

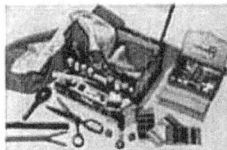

SINGER SEWING CENTERS
THERE'S ONE NEAR YOU TO SERVE YOU

1949

"SINGER Featherweight PORTABLE The World's Finest – The World's Lightest!"

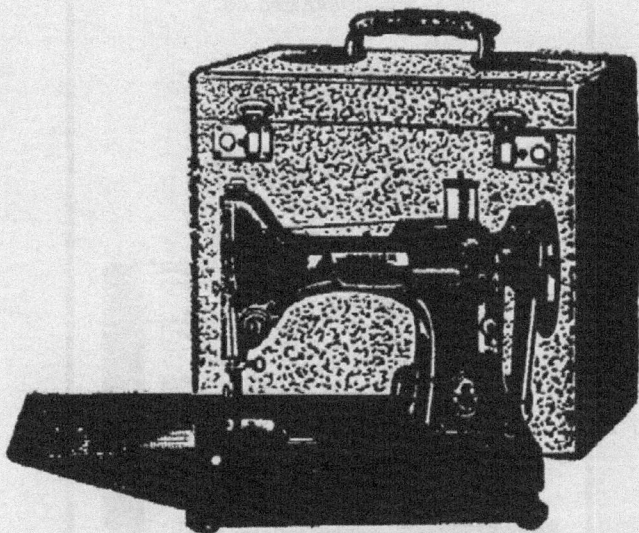

SINGER Featherweight PORTABLE
The World's Finest -- The World's Lightest!

(Only 11 lbs., 2 ozs.!)

A portable sewing machine that has all the features, and will do practically all the work, of a full size machine. So quiet and smooth running it wouldn't wake a sleeping baby!

A DISTINCTIVE GIFT, FOR HER, AT EASTER TIME

SINGER SEWING CENTER

April 1949

Look for the Red **S** on the window

*Reg. U.S. Pat. Off.
by THE SINGER MFG. CO.

IMMEDIATE DELIVERY

BRAND NEW

SINGER

Featherweight
Portable **$145**

● Weight 11 lbs., 1 oz.

● Complete Course in
Home Dress Making
Given Without Charge

SINGER
SEWING MACHINE CO.

April 1949

24

"This Christmas there'll be _Singers_ under the Tree!"

December 1949

"THE SMARTEST SANTAS SHOP AT
SINGER SEWING CENTERS!"

December 1949

1950 - 1959

"Dress beautifully and cut clothing costs in half!"

1950

"Smart summer clothes – way _below_ store prices..."

Summer 1950

"Have clothes that look <u>twice</u> the price!"

"WARNING! Sewing Machine Buyers!
Buy now and Avoid the Stock Shortages
That Appear To Be Inevitable!"

August 1950

"Once in her life... every woman should have the thrill of a SINGER Christmas!"

December 1950

"Now – finest, most beautiful
SINGER SEWING MACHINES
in 99 Christmases!"

December 1950

"Make beautiful clothes at beautiful savings!"

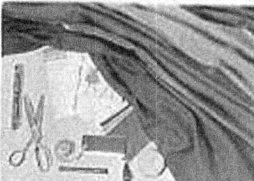

1951

"One hundred years of beautiful sewing prove SINGER IS YOUR BEST BUY!"

1951

A charming Early American Cabinet

A beautiful cabinet tailored to fit your FEATHERWEIGHT*! Here is a distinctive piece of period furniture made of carefully selected American Maple in the lovely Colonial manner.

The Colonial Cabinet and FEATHERWEIGHT Portable combine both luxury and efficiency.

The FEATHERWEIGHT lifts easily into position when you're ready to sew. And you can remove it so quickly and easily for travelling.

Desired stitch length obtained by handy lever.

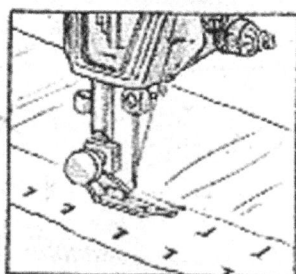

Hinged foot sews over pins and bulky seams.

Bobbin cas for repl

1951 Brochure (left page)

36

for your FEATHERWEIGHT *Portable*

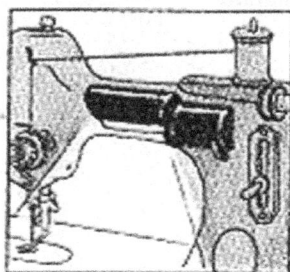

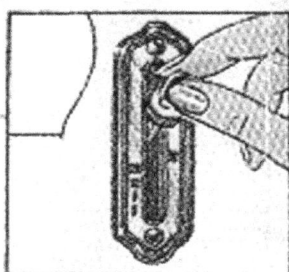

ily accessible
acement.

SINGER* Light floods work
with proper light.

Sews forward or backward
with flick of lever.

1951 Brochure (right page)

SINGER* Utility Tables *for the*

FEATHERWEIGHT fits easily into recess. For smooth table top, panel may be replaced.

Provides a fine surface fo[r] Its good looks make it hand[y]

For extra working space, add an extension table ... slips right onto your utility table.

Table combination has ma[ny] cially good for buffet servi[ng]

Numbered dial to regulate tension easily, accurately.

Electric bobbin-winder saves precious time.

Foot control range of se[w]

1951 Brochure (left page)

FEATHERWEIGHT *Portable*

r card-playing.
dy for teas, too.

A versatile, convenient table. Easy-folding metal legs. Handsome wood top has a removable panel to accommodate your FEATHERWEIGHT. An attractive SINGER* stool with tray under cushion for your sewing accessories is the finishing touch for this complete sewing ensemble.

ny uses. Espe-
ce and games.

governs wide
wing speeds.

Motor quiet, dependable,
fully enclosed.

Folding leaf provides
extra sewing space.

1951 Brochure (right page)

1951 Model 222 Brochure

In 1951, the SINGER FEATHERWEIGHT PORTABLE was the most popular model in the US with the National average price around $137.50

SINGER FEATHERWEIGHT

PORTABLE

ONLY
$145.00

EASY BUDGET TERMS

LIBERAL

TRADE-IN ALLOWANCE

INCLUDING * CARRYING CASE
* Basic Set of Singer Attachments
* Course of 8 Sewing Lessons
* Singer Warranty

SHOP EARLY
AVOID THE CHRISTMAS RUSH!

Singer Sewing Center

November 1951

"GIVE HER THE GIFT OF A LIFETIME... A NEW SINGER SEWING MACHINE!"

December 1951

"THERE'S NO GRANDER GIFT TO GIVE OR GET A SINGER SEWING MACHINE"

THERE'S NO GRANDER **GIFT** TO GIVE OR TO GET A SINGER SEWING MACHINE

Such a Wonderful Selection---

MOTHER, WIFE OR SISTER

Finest SINGERS Ever!

PRICES FROM

$89.50

- Easy budget terms
- Liberal trade-in allowance.

Take your choice of these beautiful new SINGER* Sewing machines! Now available for immediate delivery. Every one built for a lifetime of pleasant sewing. World's most popular, most dependable machines!

YOURS—at no extra cost with every new **SINGER!**

- Basic set of SINGER* attachments.
- Complete course in Home Dressmaking or Home Decorating.
- 5-year SINGER warranty of manufacturing perfection.

BUDGET PORTABLE is sturdy, compact, low-priced. Comes in handy case for carrying or storage.

DELUXE MODERN DESK has three roomy drawers. A handsome piece with stool to match.

GRACEFUL QUEEN ANNE MODEL adds to the charm of any room. Always a SINGER favorite.

SINGER* FEATHERWEIGHT PORTABLE weighs only 11 pounds, does work of a full-size model.

*A trade-mark of THE SINGER MANUFACTURING COMPANY

SINGER SEWING CENTER

December 1951

NO FINER
GIFT . . . . .

SINGER FEATHERWEIGHT
PORTABLE

ONLY

$149.50

Easy
Budget
Terms

•

Liberal
Trade-in
Allowance

INCLUDING * CARRYING CASE

* Basic Set Of Singer Attachments
* Course of 8 Sewing Lessons
* Singer Warranty

December 1951

THE MOST POPULAR PORTABLE IN ALL THE WORLD

The SINGER *Featherweight* PORTABLE SEWING MACHINE

1951 Brochure

1951 Brochure

A Century of SINGER *Leadership is behind the* FEATHERWEIGHT *Portable*

At last here is a machine designed to be carried *easily*. So light in weight, so free of noise and vibration, yet it has all the features of a full-sized machine. And, like all SINGER Machines, this portable beauty is precision-made to last, to give top service its whole long-lifetime. Included with the FEATHERWEIGHT is the smart black carrying case pictured above at left. Made for the machine, it also holds a set of basic SINGER Attachments, extra bobbins, needles and the foot control with generous length of cord.

Give Her a

SINGER

Featherweight
Portable
Sewing Machine
All Modern Features

149.50

Lo v Down Payment
Take 18 mos To Pay

YOUR SINGER SEWING CENTER

December 1951

"Sew at home"

Sew at home —

Upstairs or downstairs. No need to confine yourself to just one room . . . your FEATHERWEIGHT brings you right into the family circle. Precision construction makes this machine so smooth-running it can be used on any table. Perfect for small homes, apartments.

1952

"...and for my big gift"

...and for my big gift

More women will wish for—and get—a SINGER this Christmas than any other machine and here's why...

Famous SLANT-O-MATIC*. Here is the most talented machine you can buy. Just by "tuning" a knob you can create thousands of fancy stitches. Sew on buttons, darn socks, blindstitch hems, too. Cabinet, portable styles. Made in America.

New! SLANT-O-MATIC Special . . . brilliant new machine gives you many features of the SLANT-O-MATIC at a lower price. And it comes with a set of FASHION* Discs for fancy stitching. Cabinet, portable styles. Made in America.

New! SLANT-NEEDLE Deluxe. This greatest-of-all straight-stitch machines has foolproof threading; exclusive slant-needle; front "drop-in" bobbin and a zigzag attachment for fancy stitching. Cabinet, portable styles. Made in America.

Young-Budget SINGER . . . sleek new machine designed specially for young homemakers! Easy to run, comes with complete set of attachments. And, young husbands like the tiny price. Cabinet, portable styles. Made in Great Britain.

And you can tell Santa . . . SINGER low prices start at $59⁹⁹ for the SPARTAN* model.

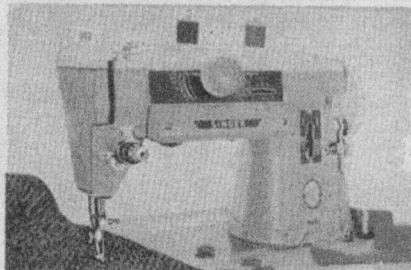

The FEATHERWEIGHT* has probably been put under more Christmas trees than any other electric portable. Weighs only 11 pounds, yet does the job of a full-size SINGER* Sewing Machine. Compact for storage, too. Made in America.

SINGER SEWING CENTERS

Also headquarters for SINGER* Vacuum Cleaners
Listed in your phone book under SINGER SEWING MACHINE CO.
*A Trademark of THE SINGER MANUFACTURING CO.

1952

48

"A present with a future... if it's a SINGER"

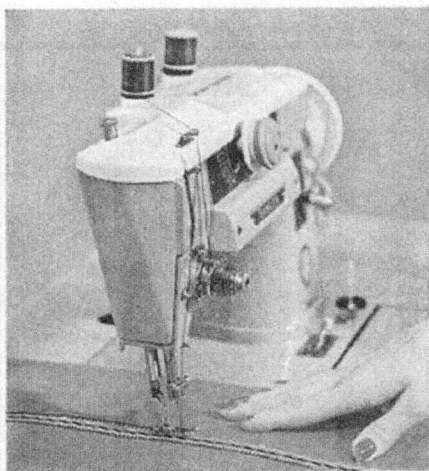

A present with a future . . . if it's a **SINGER**

The Popular Slant-Needle SINGER. Only straight-stitching machine with a needle that slants forward for easier seeing and sewing. Available with Automatic Zigzagger attachment for fancy stitching.

Streamlined Straight-Needle SINGER. Completely modern in every way—does perfect straight stitching. Like every SINGER, it's backed by over 100 years' experience in making the most dependable machines.

Famous FEATHERWEIGHT* Portable. An 11-lb. wonder that travels easily, stores easily, does the work of a full-sized SINGER even on heavy fabrics! Sturdily built with all the modern conveniences.

Extra-value SINGER Portable. Buy of a lifetime . . . to last a lifetime! Like every new SINGER, comes with *free* sewing course. SINGER machines available on easy budget terms, trade-in allowance.

New **SINGER** Slant-O-Matic...

greatest sewing machine ever built

The brilliant new Slant-O-Matic outsews all other sewing machines for both straight and fancy stitching . . . yet it's amazingly *easy* to operate.

It has 24 fabulous features, including the exclusive Slant-Needle for easier seeing, smoother sewing; an exclusive "drop-in" bobbin . . . in *front* of the needle where it's easy to reach; a built-in stitch chart that shows how to "tune in" the fancy stitch you select at the turn of a knob; gear motor drive for *stall-free* sewing.

The only automatic zigzag machine for home use made in America, the SINGER* Slant-O-Matic is built for a *lifetime* of sewing. Comes in cabinets or portable case.

A gift for every purse . . . from **SINGER**

SINGER* Sewing Boxes. A variety of fabrics, forms and colors to delight young and old alike. From $1.98.

SINGER SEWHANDY*. For the little lady on your list—a miniature SINGER that really sews! Only $9.95.

S **SINGER SEWING CENTERS**

Listed in your phone book under SINGER SEWING MACHINE CO.
*A trademark of THE SINGER MANUFACTURING COMPANY

Handsome setting for any **SINGER** . . . one of these new "Designer" Cabinets!

Early American Console. Light Honey-tone or Salem maple finish.

American Modern Desk. Blond, walnut or mahogany finish.

Modern Console. Blond or walnut finish. Richly brass-tipped.

Traditional Desk. Rich mahogany finish. Graceful tiered drawers.

Bow Front Console. Deep or casual mahogany finish. Brass pulls.

1952

49

SINGER FEATHERWEIGHT PORTABLE
PRECISION-BUILT TO LAST A LIFETIME

ONLY
$149.50

EASY BUDGET TERMS
LIBERAL
TRADE-IN ALLOWANCE

INCLUDING * CARRYING CASE
* Basic Set of Singer Attachments
* Course of 6 Sewing Lessons
* Singer Warranty

We will be happy to send a Factory Representative to your home. You will be under no obligation; or stop in at our store in person.

FOR YOUR PROTECTION SINGER sells and services its Sewing Machines and other products only through SINGER SEWING CENTERS Identified by the Red "S" Trade-mark and the "SINGER SEWING CENTER" emblem on the window, and never through department stores, dealers, or other outlets.

* A Trade Mark of THE SINGER MFG. CO.

April 1952

50

"Only SINGER offers you this complete choice!"

1953

"She'll Love SINGER Gifts"
Now only $159.00 for a Featherweight

She'll Love SINGER *gifts*

We're well stocked for Christmas here at your SINGER SEWING CENTER. Won't you stop in and see? You'll find *everything* she needs for sewing plus the two finest vacuum cleaners made. Such smart gifts…such sensible prices! Here are just a few of the many gifts we feature:

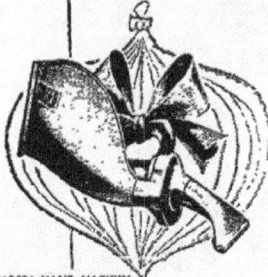

THE SINGER® HAND VACUUM
Largest-selling hand vacuum cleaner in the world! Powerful as many full-sized cleaners! Complete set of attachments available at small extra cost. **25.25**

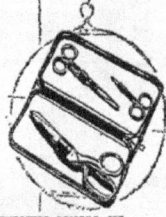

LEATHERETTE SCISSOR SET
Finest quality 7" Dressmaking Shears, 6" Sewing and 3½" Embroidery Scissors in beautiful suedine-lined case. **8.95**

IMPORTED SEA GRASS SEWING BASKET
A lovely, useful container for sewing supplies. Smart rayon lining. **3.98**

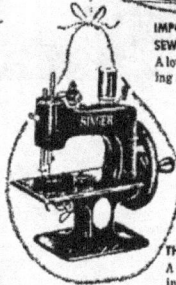

THE SEWHANDY®
A real chain-stitch SINGER® Sewing Machine — not a toy. Perfect for children because it's so safe… ideal for teaching girls to sew. **12.75**

THE SINGER® FEATHERWEIGHT® PORTABLE
Weighs only a fraction over 11 pounds, yet it can do all the work of a large-size machine. Many other models to choose from, too—. prices to fit every purse! **159.00**

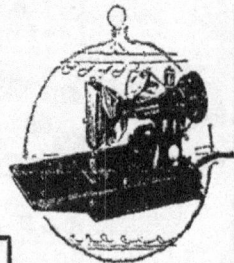

THE SINGER® VACUUM CLEANER
For greatest dirt-getting action! Complete sewing course comes as a gift with purchase of vacuum. Only $5.00 per month after minimum down payment.

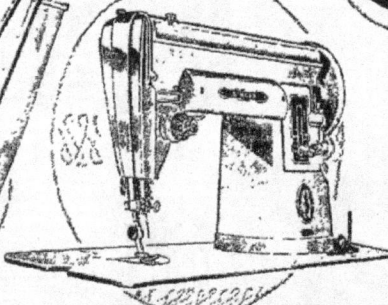

NEW 301
She'll get a whole new slant on sewing with the newest of the famous SINGER family of fine machines —the "301." Features exclusive slant-needle for the easiest, most relaxed sewing position ever. Built-in handle makes the "301" a cabinet model and portable all in one. Many other modern features. Liberal allowance on present machine, minimum down payment. Easy terms.

SEE THE BRAND NEW SINGER $**109**.50
ROUND BOBBIN PORTABLE
and ROUND BOBBIN CONSOLE **144.50**
Sews forward and backward, and over pins, also embroiders…

December 1953

Discounted to $109.95

SEWING MACHINE
SINGER
Featherweight Portable
Complete $109.95
GUARANTEED
(Will accept $2.00 a week)

February 1954

Discounted to $100.00

World Famous
SINGER
Featherweight
Portable
NOW $100
Was $159
ONLY $10^{50}
DOWN

June 1954

October 1954

54

$169.50 with a Zig-Zag Attachment

FREE!

With the Purchase
of the Famous
SINGER 11-lb.
Featherweight
Portable Sewing
Machine

The Famous Zig-Zag Attachment

- Does Embroidering—
- Does Applique—
- Does Zig Zag—
- Does Many Other Sewing Jobs

This terrific combination is offered for a limited time only at a special price of

$169.50

$15 Down—Easy Terms

SINGER SEWING CENTER

October 1954

SPECIAL OFFER
FREE
ZIG-ZAG ATTACHMENT WITH THE PURCHASE OF A SINGER
FEATHERWEIGHT PORTABLE

this...

... the wonderful SINGER* FEATHERWEIGHT Portable, a mere 11 pounds in weight, yet so sturdy. Just give it something rough and tough to sew like denim slipcovers or something fine and dainty like the sheerest of silks. No wonder it's the largest selling portable in the world.

plus this

The SINGER* Zigzag Attachment. With it your FEATHERWEIGHT* Portable will do zigzag stitching too, as well as straight sewing and decorative stitching. Here are a few of the things you can do with it.

- Applique
- Zigzagging
- Overcasting
- Inserting Lace
- Decorative Tucking
- Bar Tacking

ALL FOR AS LOW AS $15.00 DOWN
EASY TERMS

ACT SOON! — TWO WEEKS ONLY!

*A Trade Mark of THE SINGER MFG. CO.

SINGER SEWING CENTER

Listed in your telephone book only under SINGER SEWING MACHINE CO.

October 1954

56

"Put A SINGER In Santa's Bag"

December 1954

"PUT A SINGER IN SANTA'S BAG"

December 1954

58

"It's a 3-way thrill to say... I made it myself!"

It's a 3-way thrill
to say...
"I made it myself!"

SINGER SEWING CENTERS

There's a SINGER that's just right for you! Only SINGER makes them all!

1954

a few of the many special features

Desired stitch length obtained by handy lever

Hinged foot sews over pins and bulky seams

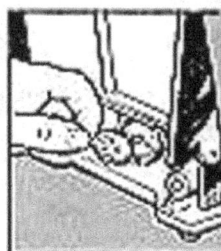

Bobbin is easily accessible for replacement

Sisagelight gives light right on the sewing

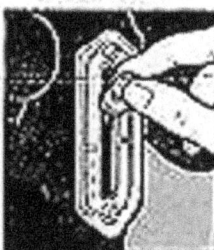

Sews forward or backward with a flick of the lever

Numbered dial facilitates accurate tension

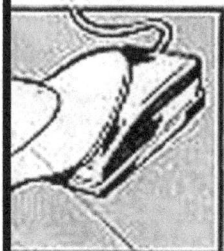

Foot control governs wide range of sewing speeds

Motor is fully enclosed, quiet and dependable

Folding leaf provides extra sewing space

1954 Brochure (left page)

60

"Has all the features and does the work of a full-sized machine."

1954 Brochure (right page)

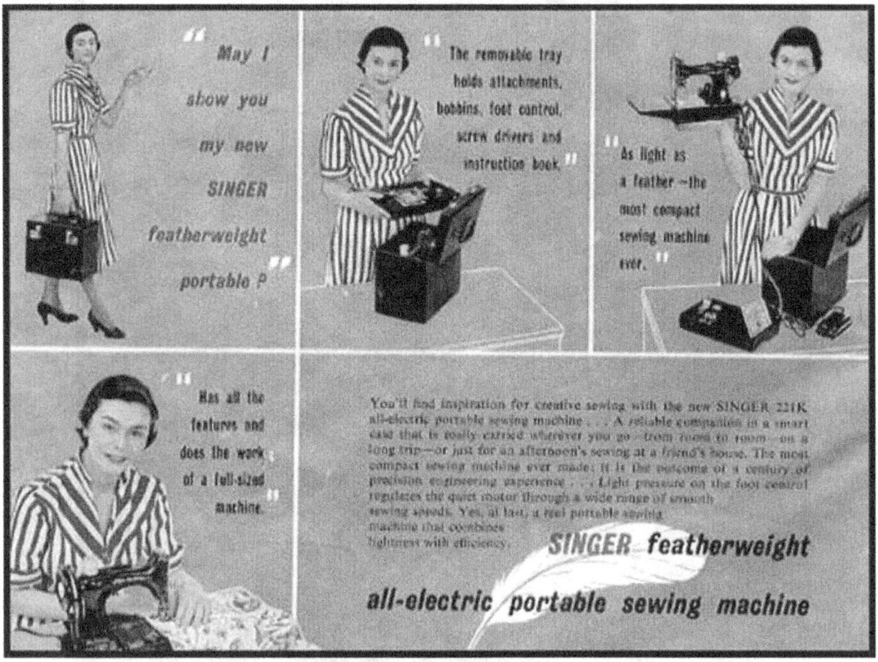

1954 Brochure

November 1955

63

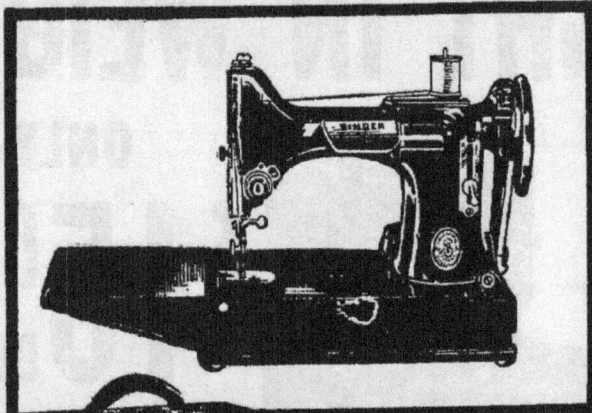

November 1956

"FOR CHRISTMAS give her this SINGER Featherweight Portable"

DEC. 25

FOR CHRISTMAS

give her this

SINGER
Featherweight Portable

$1.70

PAY AS LITTLE AS **A WEEK¹**

¹ After minimum down payment

The perfect present for her sewing future, a SINGER¹ Featherweight Portable. This handy electric portable weighs only 11 lbs., but has all the mechanical features and does the work of a full sized machine.,

It comes with a smart, convenient carrying case. . .

when you buy SINGER you buy the BEST

SINGER SEWING CENTER
Listed in the Telephone Book under SINGER SEWING MACHINE CO.

December 1956

"There's always a Singer Sewing Centre ..... where you can obtain.... a reel of cotton to a modern lightweight sewing machine..." Model 222 in foreground

Ideal Home   March, 1957

There's always a Singer Sewing Centre near you to serve you, where you can obtain every sewing aid from a reel of cotton to a modern lightweight sewing machine, and expert advice on all your sewing problems.

1957 Great Britain

"For your teen or college age daughter- a SINGER FEATHERWEIGHT Portable"

November 1957

"for her most unforgettable christmas ... give
SINGER"

November 1957

"For sewing _and_ furnishing there's the right SINGER"

For the Cottage home

For Period furnishing

For sewing _and_ furnishing there's the right SINGER

After choosing the type of machine suited to your particular sewing needs, you can decide to have either a portable or cabinet model. Of course for a flat any of the compact portables is ideal, but in the family home you may well prefer a cabinet model. Among the many styles of Singer Cabinet there is one to harmonise with your own furnishing scheme . . . closed, a beautiful occasional table, and open, an efficient sewing machine. A generous allowance will be made in part exchange for your old machine.

See the comprehensive range at your local Singer Sewing Centre

SINGER SEWING MACHINE COMPANY LIMITED, SINGER BUILDING, CITY ROAD, LONDON, E.C.1

For the Bachelor flat

For Contemporary living

1957

69

The Singer Featherweight* —makes light work of everything you sew!

An all-electric model, the Singer Featherweight 221 really does make light work of everything you sew, and like the bigger machines in the Singer range, the free fashion aids supplied with it help to give all your sewing a really finished, expert look.

A wonderfully light machine (it weighs only 11 lbs.), the Singer 221 is supplied in a compact carrying-case — which also holds the foot control, attachments, bobbins and tools.

* A Trademark of THE SINGER MANUFACTURING CO.

1959 Brochure (left page)

1959 Brochure (right page)

"Now there's a SINGER every Santa can afford"

Now there's a
SINGER
every Santa can afford

(New low prices start at only $89.50!)

The SLANT-O-MATIC—most modern automatic sigzag machine. And the easiest! Lets you "tune" knotless zigzag fancy stitches, do fine straight stitching. Built-in threading and stitch charts. Snap-in front bobbin. Cabinets, portables.

The SLANT NEEDLE—only straightstitch machine with needle slanted forward for better visibility! Simple to operate and, like all SINGER Sewing Machines, it's built for a lifetime. Adapts to Automatic Zigzagger. Consoles, desks, portables.

The FEATHERWEIGHT—world's most popular. Just 11 pounds! Does job of a full-sized SINGER, from sheerest to heaviest fabrics. Compact to store. And, of course, parts and service are always available at 1700 SINGER SEWING CENTERS.

SINGER
SEWING
CENTERS

New Young-Budget SINGER—designed especially for young homemakers! Sews backward and forward. Comes with complete set of attachments ... and you get a complete SINGER Sewing Course free! Choice of cabinet or portable styles.

Economy Portable—at a new price, the machine that was already the thriftiest value in town! Toy-bobbin model with famous SINGER light, easy threading, backtack stitch, carrying case. Ask about small down payment, easy terms!

1959

1960 - 1969

Such a versatile little machine, the Singer "Treble-Two"

Versatile, that's the word for the Singer Treble-Two. It's *all-electric*. It's portable (a real lightweight at only 12½ lbs.)—yet it does all kinds of sewing because it's *convertible*. With the flat bed in position, your 222 is ready to do *all* the sewing that a bigger machine can do. But by simply slipping off a portion of the base, you expose the tubular bed—such a help for sewing in normally hard-to-get-at places like sleeves and trouserbottoms, or for patching and darning.

The Treble-Two comes in a trim black carrying-case, which also holds the foot control, attachments, bobbins and tools.

1960 Model 222 Brochure (left page)

74

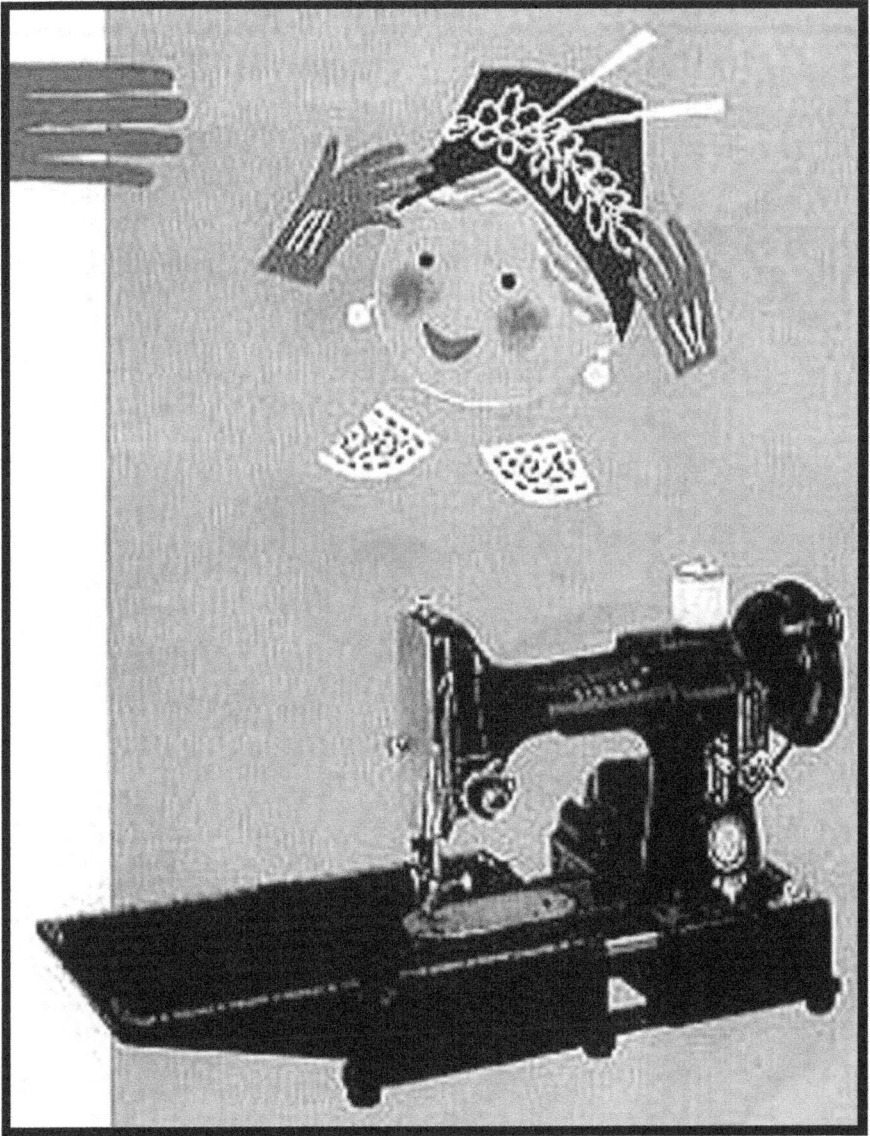

1960 Model 222 Brochure (right page)

"Persuasive things to say when hinting for your SINGER"

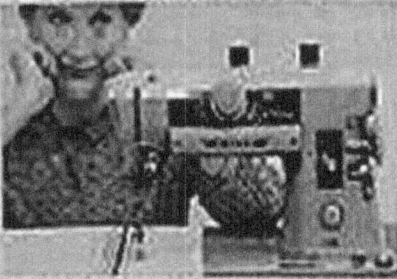

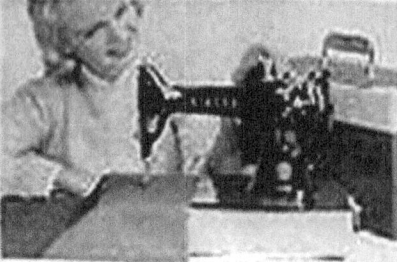

1960

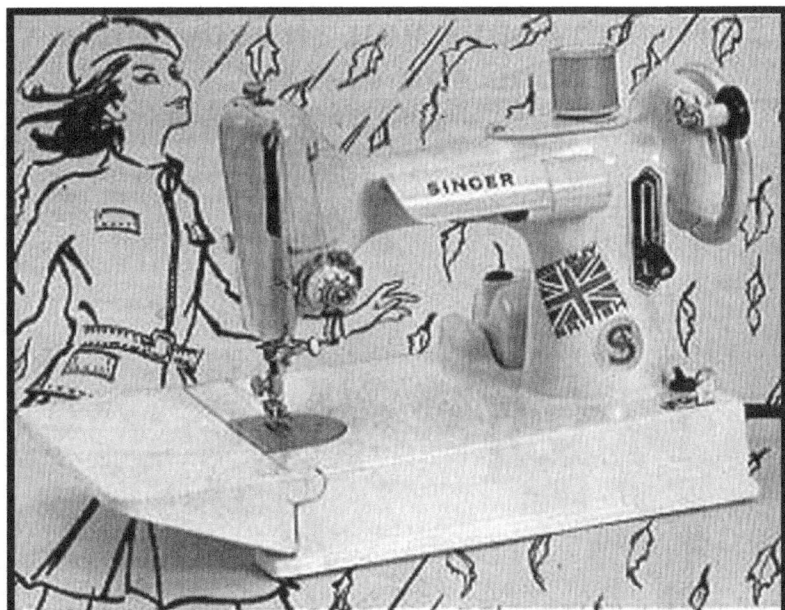

The British-made 'featherweight' 221

weighs only 12-1/2 lbs. in its sturdy carry-case -you can easily take it in the pub. Finished to fine tolerances, the 221 thrives on hard work, does not only beautiful straight stitching on all materials,but inserts zippers,does cording, piping, bias bonding, darning and free-hand embroidery. The 221 has a smooth rotary action and a quiet fully-suppressed motor.Stitch length is variable from 6 to 30 stitches to the inch. The single-turn tension control is calibrated. The 'featherweight' 221 has a practical extension leaf and the sewing light is seperately switched. There's a quick bobbin winder and a hinged presser foot and a built-in threadcutter.

1962

"P.S. Mommy says you already know the one she wants"

"P. S. Mommy says you already know the one she wants".

1962 Christmas (left page)

"P.S. Mommy says you already know the one she wants"

1962 Christmas (right page)

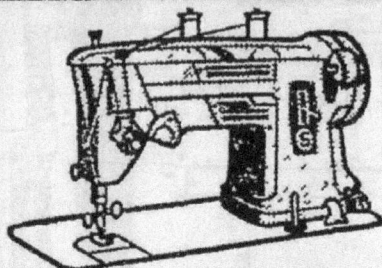

NEW Featherweight
PORTABLE
Sewing Machine

Reg. 149.50
NOW .... 99^{50}

Reg. $17.95 TRANSISTOR RADIO included at no extra cost!

STYLE-O-MATIC* Zigzag
139^{50}

Save substantially on sewing machine heads from demonstrators and floor models. You'll find popular straight stitching or zig-zag machines. The selection of these is limited, so plan to come early for the best choice.

†after a small down payment on our Easy Budget Plan

SINGER SEWING CENTERS
HEADQUARTERS FOR ALL YOUR SEWING AND FLOOR CARE NEEDS

Listed in your phone book under SINGER SEWING MACHINE CO.

July 1963

Most portable portable
The *Featherweight** sewing
machine Compact, weighs
only 11 lbs , yet it's a real
"work horse." $149.95 with case

November 1964

81

FEATHERWEIGHT*
Sewing Machine
by SINGER

World's most portable portable! Less than 12 lbs., yet sews everything beautifully!

$149^{95}

with case
EASY TERMS

December 1964

Gifts
for Her

Most portable portable
The Featherweight sewing
machine Compact, weighs
only 11 lbs, yet it's a real
"work horse" $149 95
with case

SINGER SEWING CO

December 1964

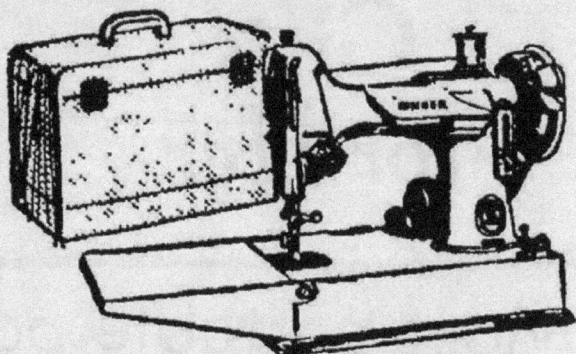

GO

SAVE $20

...on the famous FEATHERWEIGHT*
sewing machine by **SINGER**

Now in pearl white
- Less than 12 pounds
- Sews everything from
  sheers to suitings
- Sews forward and reverse

$129⁹⁵

reg. $149.95

May 1965

June 1965

August 1966

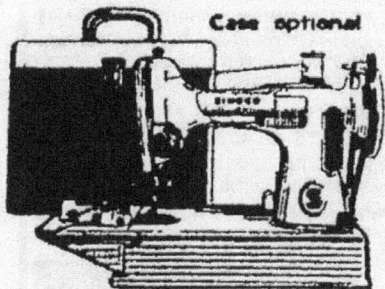
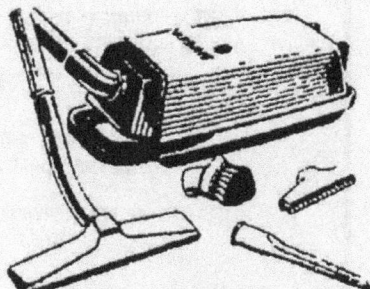

September 1966

November 1966

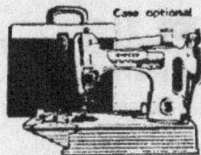
December 1966

"A dozen dandy reasons to shop Singer first!"

A dozen dandy reasons to shop Singer first!

PLUS Free gift wrapping and Free delivery in time for Christmas! Easy terms. No monthly payments till Feb. '67.

FEATHERWEIGHT* sewing machine by SINGER $129⁹⁵
An 11 lb. portable that sews all fabric weights, forward and reverse. Case included.

(model 237)
SINGER* Zig-zag sewing machine $99⁹⁵ Case included
Sews zig-zag to overcast, sew elastic. Darns, mends, embroiders without attachments.

(model HE 2700)
SINGER* Portable phono $19⁹⁵
It's battery-powered, fully-transistorized. Weighs only 4 lbs. and plays 2 speeds.

December 1966

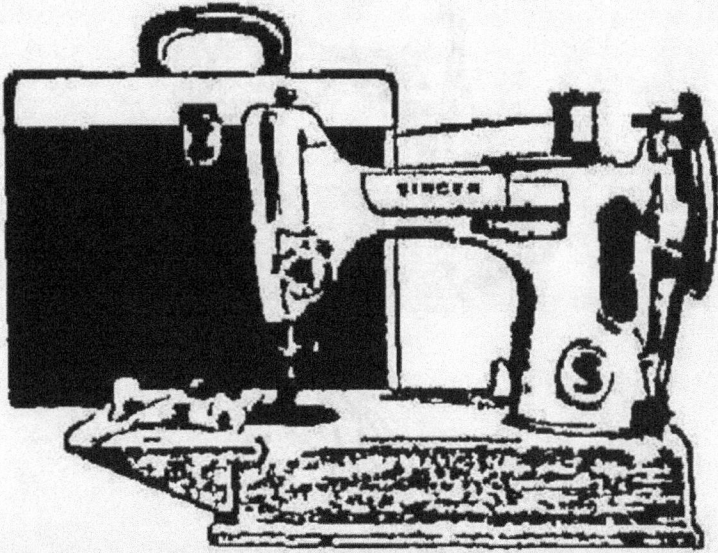

FEATHERWEIGHT*
sewing machine
by SINGER

$129⁹⁵

An 11 lb. portable that sews
all fabric weights, forward and
reverse. Case included.

January 1967

FEATHERWEIGHT SEWING MACHINE BY SINGER

• Petite, compact, distinctive design • Extremely light weight [11 lbs. 4 oz.] • Noise-free, steady, vibrationless • Easy, simple operation • The ultimate in portability

$119 95

carrying case, $10, optional extra.

February 1967

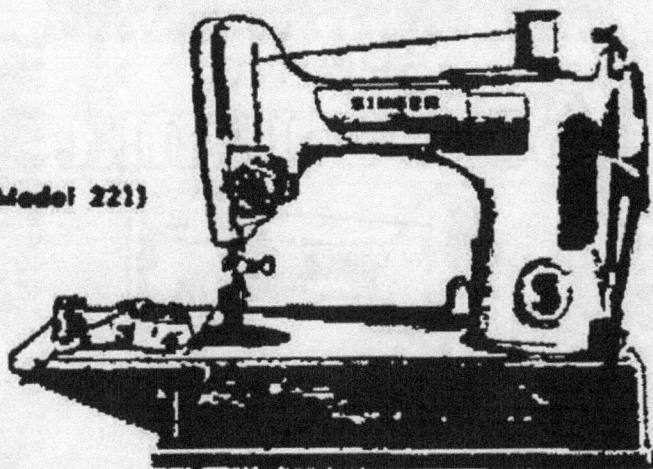

(Model 221)

FEATHERWEIGHT'
sewing machine
by SINGER

An 11 lb. portable that sews all fabric weights, forward and reverse. Carrying case $10 extra.

$99⁹⁵

March 1967

March 1967

June 1967

95

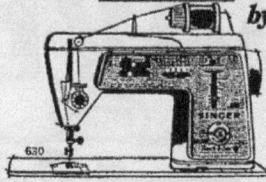

September 1968

Don't wait.

$30 OFF reg. price [221]
FEATHERWEIGHT* portable
sewing machine by Singer.
Regularly 129. NOW 99

Lightweight, only 11½ pounds, easy to tote.

NOW ONLY $88

Singer* sewing machine [229/573]
in "Lexington" cabinet.
Heavy duty, sews on all types of fabrics.
Quiet, smooth sewing, forward and reverse.

ASK ABOUT OUR CREDIT PLAN—DESIGNED TO FIT YOUR BUDGET.

What's new for tomorrow is at SINGER today!*

SINGER

For address of store nearest you,
see white pages of phone book under SINGER COMPANY.

*A Trademark of THE SINGER COMPANY

February 1969

IT'S A MONSTER SALE AT SINGER

YOUR CHOICE $88

FASHION MATE* zig-zag sewing machine by SINGER with case Sews buttonholes, buttons; darns, mends, monograms without attachments.

237/575

221/548

239/675

FEATHERWEIGHT* sewing machine by SINGER
Sews everything from sheers to sturdy leathers—smoothly, quietly. Weighs only 11½ lbs.!
Regular price $129.95.

FASHION MATE* sewing machine by SINGER in "Lexington" cabinet
Enjoy smooth stitching on all fabrics, forward and reverse. Stores in Early American cabinet.

April 1969

LAST 3 DAYS

"Monster"
SALE
at Singer's

New Zig-Zag
Sewing Machine
BUTTONHOLES-MONOGRAMS
SEWS BUTTONS

Now $88

Famous Singer
Featherweight
Portable
WAS PRICED AT $129 95

Now $88

● ● ●

for "Monster" Values
Stop at your

SINGER
SEWING CENTER

May 1969

1970 - 1973

STAND OUT Gifts for Grads

SINGER FEATHERWEIGHT SEWING MACHINE

ONE WEEK ONLY

**WEIGHS ONLY 11 LBS.
IN PORTABLE CASE
REG. $129.95**

$109⁹⁵

May 1970

And the last one – Also the lowest price!

December 1973

I hope you enjoyed this book. If you want to read more about the SINGER 221/222, check out another of my books

"the Featherweight Patents"

at my website

www.DarrelKaiserBooks.com

Please email any and all comments to

<u>Dar-Bet@att.net</u>

Made in the USA
Monee, IL
01 December 2024

71838464R00066